W9-BVP-690

EXPLORING COUNTRIES

Italy

by Walter Simmons

BLASTOFF!
5
READERS

BELLWETHER MEDIA • MINNEAPOLIS, MN

Note to Librarians, Teachers, and Parents:

Blastoff! Readers are carefully developed by literacy experts and combine standards-based content with developmentally appropriate text.

Level 1 provides the most support through repetition of high-frequency words, light text, predictable sentence patterns, and strong visual support.

Level 2 offers early readers a bit more challenge through varied simple sentences, increased text load, and less repetition of high-frequency words.

Level 3 advances early-fluent readers toward fluency through increased text and concept load, less reliance on visuals, longer sentences, and more literary language.

Level 4 builds reading stamina by providing more text per page, increased use of punctuation, greater variation in sentence patterns, and increasingly challenging vocabulary.

Level 5 encourages children to move from "learning to read" to "reading to learn" by providing even more text, varied writing styles, and less familiar topics.

Whichever book is right for your reader, Blastoff! Readers are the perfect books to build confidence and encourage a love of reading that will last a lifetime!

This edition first published in 2011 by Bellwether Media, Inc.

No part of this publication may be reproduced in whole or in part without written permission of the publisher. For information regarding permission, write to Bellwether Media, Inc., Attention: Permissions Department, 5357 Penn Avenue South, Minneapolis, MN 55419.

Library of Congress Cataloging-in-Publication Data

Simmons, Walter (Walter G.)
Italy / by Walter Simmons.
  p. cm. – (Exploring countries) (Blastoff! Readers)
Includes bibliographical references and index.
 Summary: "Developed by literacy experts for students in grades three through seven, this book introduces young readers to the geography and culture of Italy"–Provided by publisher.
 ISBN 978-1-60014-485-1 (hardcover : alk. paper)
 1. Italy–Juvenile literature. 2. Italy–Social life and customs–Juvenile literature. I. Title.
DG451.S558 2011
945–dc22   2010015685

Printed in the United States of America, North Mankato, MN.

080110   1162

Contents

Italy is a nation in southern Europe that covers 116,348 square miles (301,340 square kilometers). In the north, Italy borders France, Switzerland, Austria, and Slovenia. The rest of Italy covers a long **peninsula** that stretches into the Mediterranean Sea. This region includes the independent nations of San Marino and Vatican City. Vatican City is located in Rome, which is the capital of Italy.

Greece

East of the Italian Peninsula is the Adriatic Sea, and to the west is the Tyrrhenian Sea. The Ionian Sea separates the coastlines of Italy and Greece. Several Mediterranean islands, including Sardinia and Elba, also belong to Italy. Sicily, Italy's largest island, lies across the Strait of Messina.

5

Italy has mountains, river valleys, plains, and long seacoasts. The Apennine Mountains run through the center of the country. The peaks of the steep Alps and Dolomites rise in the north. Italy shares the slopes of Monte Bianco, or White Mountain, with France. With a height of 15,770 feet (4,807 meters), this mountain is the tallest in Europe. It is one of the few mountains in Italy that is tall enough for **glaciers** to cover its peak.

Italy has many rivers. The Po is the longest river in Italy. It waters a wide, **fertile** valley in the north and empties into the Adriatic Sea. The Arno flows through the center of Florence, and the Tiber travels through Rome.

Dolomites

Mount Vesuvius, the only active volcano on Europe's mainland, rises near the city of Naples. Its most famous eruption happened almost 2,000 years ago during the time of the **Roman Empire**. Hot ash from the volcano buried Pompeii and other nearby cities.

The ash preserved many of Pompeii's streets, shops, and temples. **Archaeologists** have dug up a large part of the city so that visitors can walk through it. Today, Pompeii looks much like it did 2,000 years ago. Vesuvius has not erupted since 1944. If it erupts again, the more than 3 million people living near its slopes will be in danger.

fun fact

Archaeologists uncovered ancient Roman bakeries along with the ruins of temples and houses. They even found bread that was baking in the ovens when Mount Vesuvius erupted!

Pompeii temple ruins

porcupine

Italy is home to many kinds of wildlife. Porcupines, red deer, hares, and wolves roam in the Apennine Mountains. **Chamois** and black bears wander through the Alps. The marmot, a kind of squirrel that lives in the ground, can be found throughout the mountainous regions of Italy.

Thousands of wild boars live in the forests and mountains of Italy. With their powerful tusks, they dig in the soil for tasty insects, small animals, and roots. Farmers don't like boars destroying their fields, so a busy boar-hunting season begins late in the fall.

pink flamingos

chamois

wild boar

Many different birds and ocean animals inhabit the islands and waters of Italy. On Sardinia, pink flamingos nest in coastal **wetlands**. Hawks and eagles **migrate** to Sicily and southern Italy in the spring. Sharks, tuna, dolphins, and swordfish swim in the seas around Italy.

Around 58 million people live in Italy. Italians have **ancestors** from the regions in and around modern Italy. Many **immigrants** have come to Italy from Albania, Greece, Morocco, Romania, and recently China. These immigrants have brought their customs and languages with them to Italy.

Today, most Italians live in the northern part of the country. Southern Italy, known as the *Mezzogiorno*, has fewer big cities than the north. Almost all Italians speak Italian, the country's official language.

Speak Italian!

English	Italian	How to say it
hello	ciao	chow
good-bye	ciao	chow
yes	si	see
no	no	no
please	per favore	pehr fah-VOHR-eh
thank you	grazie	GRAHT-zee-eh
friend (male)	amico	ah-MEE-ko
friend (female)	amica	ah-MEE-ka

Most Italians live in large cities. Cars, taxis, buses, and motorbikes crowd city streets in Italy as people rush to work or school. In the countryside, life moves at a slower pace. Once or twice a day, farmers visit the nearest town or village to shop and chat with friends.

Did you know?

Most Italians belong to the Roman Catholic Church. Every city and village has at least one church, usually in the center of town. Every day, bells ring to call people to mass.

Where People Live in Italy

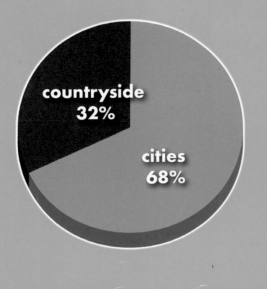

countryside
32%

cities
68%

Many people enjoy walking through the streets and **plazas**, or *piazzas*, of Italy's cities. They visit shops that sell shoes, clothing, food, or newspapers and books. In the evening, families gather together for a meal. This is the day's most important event. Afterward, they may enjoy a show on television or go out to see a movie.

In Italy, everyone starts school when they are 6 years old, and they must attend until they are 16. Students spend their first year in *scuola materna*, or kindergarten. Then they attend elementary school, or *scuola elementare*, where they study math, science, Italian, history, and geography. Elementary school lasts for five years.

Middle school, or *scuola media*, follows and lasts for three years. Students continue with math and Italian and begin to study foreign languages as well as art, drama, and music. If they wish to go on to high school, they must pass an exam. If they pass, they choose between high schools that prepare them for university or high schools that prepare them for specific jobs.

fun fact

The University of Bologna is the oldest university in Europe. It is thought that classes began meeting there in 1088. That was more than 900 years ago!

Where People Work in Italy

manufacturing
30.7%

farming
4.2%

services 65.1%

Did you know?

Ferrari is an Italian car company that was started in 1929. The Ferrari Enzo can reach speeds up to 225 miles (362 kilometers) per hour. Only 400 Enzos were ever made.

Italy is one of the most productive countries in the world. In cities, factory workers make tires, machinery, and chemicals. Some of the world's fastest sports cars are designed and made in Italy. There are also thousands of small workshops where Italians make clothing, shoes, and handbags. Many Italians have **service jobs**. They work in banks, hospitals, and schools. Workers in retail stores, hotels, and restaurants also serve the millions of tourists who visit Italy every year.

Much of the farming in Italy is done in the Po River Valley. Farmers grow wheat, rice, tomatoes, and grapes. Southern Italy has many **orchards** where olive, **fig**, and citrus trees are grown.

fun fact

Italy had a professional basketball league in 1920, more than 25 years before the National Basketball Association (NBA) formed in the United States.

Italians spend much of their free time playing sports. The most popular sport in Italy is *calcio*, or soccer. Basketball is another favorite of Italians. They call the sport *pallacanestro*. People in Italy also enjoy traveling around their country. Adventurous Italians cycle, camp, or hike through Italy's rugged landscape.

There are also many historic sites and beautiful churches to visit in Italy. Museums display some of the world's most famous works of art by Italian painters and sculptors. Many Italians enjoy going to shows, especially movies and plays. **Opera**, a type of dramatic play set to music, was invented in Italy.

opera

fun fact

The average Italian eats more than 60 pounds (27.2 kilograms) of pasta every year.

Italian food is rich and filling. Pasta is part of almost every meal. It comes in many different shapes. In the north, people also eat a rice dish called *risotto*. Many Italian dishes are prepared with olive oil.

For most Italians, breakfast is a light meal of bread or pastries served with coffee. Lunch is a midday snack. People crowd small shops that sell pizza, pasta, or *calzones*, which combine meat, cheese, and vegetables inside a crust. Dinner is the largest meal of the day and is eaten late in the evening. It includes soup, salad, one or two main courses, and dessert. *Gelato* is an Italian dessert similar to ice cream, but it is heavier and has a stronger flavor. Many adults enjoy espresso after dinner.

gelato

calzone

! fun fact

Italians celebrate *Carnevale* a few months before Easter. The town of Viareggio is famous for its large floats and magnificent parades.

On national holidays, Italians get time off from work or school. Many of these holidays, such as Easter and Christmas, are religious holidays. Most Italians are Roman **Catholic**. August 15 is *Ferragosto*, or the Feast of the Assumption. This holiday honors the Virgin Mary, an important figure to Catholics.

Other holidays celebrate Italy's history. On April 25, the country celebrates the end of World War II with Liberation Day. **Republic** Day, on June 2, marks the day in 1946 when Italians voted to establish a republic. On this day, Rome and other cities throw grand parades.

Ferragosto

One of the most famous cities in Italy is Venice. It rises in the middle of a large **lagoon**. To escape an invasion, the ancient Venetians built their city on top of 117 small islands. They established a republic that lasted for over 1,000 years before Venice became part of Italy.

There are no cars in Venice. People get around on foot or by boat. Motorboats and **gondolas** travel up and down about 150 small **canals**. The Grand Canal is the main waterway of Venice. Narrow walkways are lined with shops and houses that are hundreds of years old. Piazza San Marco is the heart of Venice. Millions of tourists visit it every year to learn about Italian art, history, and culture.

! fun fact
Venice has over 400 bridges, 3,000 alleys, and 450 souvenir shops.

Venice has a problem with *acqua alta*, or high water. Once in a while, the sea floods the entire city. To stay dry, people must walk on temporary wooden sidewalks.

Fast Facts About Italy

Italy's Flag

The flag of Italy is made up of three vertical bands. The bands are green, white, and red. The colors come from old emblems of Milan, a city in northern Italy. The government of Italy officially adopted the flag in 1948, after the modern republic was founded.

Official Name: Italian Republic

Area: 116,348 square miles (301,340 square kilometers); Italy is the 71st largest country in the world.

Capital City:	Rome
Important Cities:	Milan, Naples, Turin, Florence, Venice, Genoa, Bologna
Population:	58,090,681 (July 2010)
Official Language:	Italian
National Holiday:	Republic Day (June 2)
Religions:	Christian (90%), Other (10%)
Major Industries:	farming, manufacturing, services, tourism
Natural Resources:	coal, iron ore, marble, mercury, natural gas, zinc
Manufactured Products:	appliances, cars, clothing, food products, machinery, steel, chemicals
Farm Products:	cheese, citrus fruits, corn, wheat, grapes, olives, rice, tomatoes, figs, wine
Unit of Money:	euro; the euro is divided into 100 cents.

Glossary

ancestors—relatives who lived long ago

archaeologists—scientists who study the remains of past civilizations

canals—trenches dug across land that connect two bodies of water; canals allow ships to move between the two bodies of water.

Catholic—a member of the Roman Catholic Church; Roman Catholics are Christian.

chamois—animals that are similar to antelope and goats; chamois live in the mountains of Italy.

fertile—supports growth

fig—a sweet fruit that can be eaten fresh or dried

glaciers—massive sheets of ice that move slowly over large areas of land

gondolas—long wooden boats designed to move easily through the canals of Venice

immigrants—people who leave one country to live in another country

lagoon—a large, shallow pool of seawater fed by the ocean

migrate—to move from one place to another, often with the seasons

opera—a dramatic play set to music and performed by singers and an orchestra

orchards—fields of fruit-bearing trees

peninsula—a section of land that extends out from a larger piece of land and is almost completely surrounded by water

plazas—public squares; the Italian word for plaza is *piazza*.

republic—a nation governed by elected leaders instead of a monarch

Roman Empire—an ancient civilization that ruled over much of Europe, the Middle East, and North Africa

service jobs—jobs that perform tasks for people or businesses

wetlands—wet, spongy land; bogs, marshes, and swamps are wetlands.

To Learn More

AT THE LIBRARY

Bingham, Jane. *Italy*. Minneapolis, Minn.: Clara House Books, 2010.

Harvey, Miles. *Look What Came from Italy*. New York, N.Y.: Franklin Watts, 1998.

Petersen, Christine and David. *Italy*. New York, N.Y.: Children's Press, 2001.

ON THE WEB

Learning more about Italy is as easy as 1, 2, 3.

1. Go to www.factsurfer.com.

2. Enter "Italy" into the search box.

3. Click the "Surf" button and you will see a list of related Web sites.

With factsurfer.com, finding more information is just a click away.

Index

The images in this book are reproduced through the courtesy of: Scott Truesdale, front cover, p. 15; Maisei Raman, front cover (flag), p. 28; Giovanni Epparcello, pp. 4-5; Masahiro Sato/Photononstop/Photolibrary, pp. 6-7; Natalia Barsukova, p. 6 (small); DEA/S AMANTINI/Photolibrary, p. 8; Juan Martinez, pp. 9, 24-25, 26-27, 29 (bill); Tony Rix, pp. 10-11; Pressurepics, p. 11 (top); Radovan Spurny, p. 11 (middle); Bruno Manunza/Photolibrary, p. 11 (bottom); Image Source/Getty Images, p. 12; Tommaso Di Girolamo/Photolibrary, p. 14; Glowimages RM/Alamy, pp. 16-17; Oksana Perkins, p. 18; ableimages/Alamy, p. 19 (left); MARKA/Alamy, p. 19 (right); Getty Images, p. 20; ASSOCIATED PRESS, p. 21, 21 (small); Noam Armonn, p. 22; Dallas Events Inc, p. 23 (left); Brandon Bohling, p. 23 (right); Robert Harding Picture Library Ltd/Alamy, p. 25 (small); Tomo Jesenicnik, p. 29 (coin).

A Note to Parents and Caregivers:

Read-it! Readers are for children who are just starting on the amazing road to reading. These beautiful books support both the acquisition of reading skills and the love of books.

 The PURPLE LEVEL presents basic topics and objects using high frequency words and simple language patterns.

 The RED LEVEL presents familiar topics using common words and repeating sentence patterns.

 The BLUE LEVEL presents new ideas using a larger vocabulary and varied sentence structure.

 The YELLOW LEVEL presents more challenging ideas, a broad vocabulary, and wide variety in sentence structure.

 The GREEN LEVEL presents more complex ideas, an extended vocabulary range, and expanded language structures.

 The ORANGE LEVEL presents a wide range of ideas and concepts using challenging vocabulary and complex language structures.

When sharing a book with your child, read in short stretches, pausing often to talk about the pictures. Have your child turn the pages and point to the pictures and familiar words. And be sure to reread favorite stories or parts of stories.

There is no right or wrong way to share books with children. Fir to read with your child, and pass on the legacy of literacy.

Adria F. Klein, Ph.D.
Professor Emeritus
California State University
San Bernardino, California

_or: Christianne Jones
_signer: Amy Muehlenhardt
_age Production: Lori Bye
Creative Director: Keith Griffin
Editorial Director: Carol Jones
The illustrations in this book were created with acrylics.

Picture Window Books
5115 Excelsior Boulevard
Suite 232
Minneapolis, MN 55416
877-845-8392
www.picturewindowbooks.com

Printed in the United States of America.

Library of Congress Cataloging-in-Publication Data
Donahue, Jill L.
Rudy helps out / by Jill L. Donahue ; illustrated by Stacey Previn.
p. cm. — (Read-it! readers)
Summary: Rudy and his mother spend the day cleaning the house.
ISBN-13: 978-1-4048-2420-1 (hardcover)
ISBN-10: 1-4048-2420-0 (hardcover)
[1. House cleaning—Fiction. 2. Mothers and sons—Fiction. 3. Hispanic
Americans—Fiction. 4. Stories in rhyme.] I. Previn, Stacey, ill. II. Title. III. Series.

PZ8.3.D730Rud 2006
[E]—dc22   2006003416

Rudy Helps Out

by Jill L. Donahue

illustrated by Stacey Previn

Special thanks to our advisers for their expertise:

Adria F. Klein, Ph.D.
Professor Emeritus, California State University
San Bernardino, California

Susan Kesselring, M.A.
Literacy Educator
Rosemount–Apple Valley–Eagan (Minnesota) School District

PiCTURE WiNDOW BOOKS
Minneapolis, Minnesota

It's housecleaning day for Rudy and his mother.
It's time to get busy and help one another.

Rudy is a good worker. His mom always says so. He loves to help out and go, go, go!

6

While Mom goes to the closet to get a rag,
Rudy takes the clothes out of the laundry bag.

8

Mom scrubs the windows until they really shine. Rudy folds clothes and piles them in a line.

Rudy bends over to pick up the piles. Mom sits down to go through her files.

Mom sorts her papers and pays the bills.
Rudy starts to dust the windowsills.

13

Rudy cleans the halls with his favorite broom. Mom puts on gloves and heads to the bathroom.

Rudy and his mom are on quite a roll.
Together they scrub out the toilet bowl!

17

After they take turns mopping the floor,
Mom knows there's just one thing more.

She checks on the cookies that are baking.
She can't wait to show Rudy what she's
been making.

But where is Rudy now that the work is done?

Oh, no! Rudy is sleeping! He's too tired to have fun.

More *Read-it!* Readers

Bright pictures and fun stories help you practice your reading skills. Look for more books at your level.

Bamboo at the Beach 1-4048-1035-8

The Best Lunch 1-4048-1578-3

Clinks the Robot 1-4048-1579-1

Eight Enormous Elephants 1-4048-0054-9

Flynn Flies High 1-4048-0563-X

Freddie's Fears 1-4048-0056-5

Loop, Swoop, and Pull! 1-4048-1611-9

Marvin, the Blue Pig 1-4048-0564-8

Mary and the Fairy 1-4048-0066-2

Megan Has to Move 1-4048-1613-5

Moo! 1-4048-0643-1

My Favorite Monster 1-4048-1029-3

Pippin's Big Jump 1-4048-0555-9

Pony Party 1-4048-1612-7

The Snow Dance 1-4048-2421-9

Sounds Like Fun 1-4048-0649-0

The Ticket 1-4048-2423-5

Tired of Waiting 1-4048-0650-4

Whose Birthday Is It? 1-4048-0554-0

Looking for a specific title or level? A complete list of *Read-it!* Readers is available on our Web site:

www.picturewindowbooks.com